The Journey of Spiritual Empowerment

Liz Roberts

BALBOA.PRESS

A DIVISION OF HAY HOUSE

Balboa Press books may be ordered through booksellers or by contacting:

Balboa Press
A Division of Hay House
1663 Liberty Drive
Bloomington, IN 47403
www.balboapress.co.uk
UK TFN: 0800 0148647 (Toll Free inside the UK)
UK Local: (02) 0369 56325 (+44 20 3695 6325 from outside the UK)

Because of the dynamic nature of the Internet, any web addresses or links contained in this book may have changed since publication and may no longer be valid. The views expressed in this work are solely those of the author and do not necessarily reflect the views of the publisher, and the publisher hereby disclaims any responsibility for them.

The author of this book does not dispense medical advice or prescribe the use of any technique as a form of treatment for physical, emotional, or medical problems without the advice of a physician, either directly or indirectly. The intent of the author is only to offer information of a general nature to help you in your quest for emotional and spiritual well-being. In the event you use any of the information in this book for yourself, which is your constitutional right, the author and the publisher assume no responsibility for your actions.

Any people depicted in stock imagery provided by Getty Images are models, and such images are being used for illustrative purposes only. Certain stock imagery © Getty Images.

Print information available on the last page.

ISBN: 978-1-9822-8837-2 (sc)
ISBN: 978-1-9822-8836-5 (e)

Library of Congress Control Number: 2024904690

Balboa Press rev. date: 03/05/2024

CONTENTS

FOREWORD

Many factors influence who we are and how each part of our lives will unfold, including trauma, people we meet, and the tiny, barbed comments that sit within our shadow side for many years. All too often, it is a path filled with obstacles and challenges, making it relatively easy to give up or drift along. Then we realise years have flown by and what happened to our hopes and dreams; how do you suddenly change and make them a reality? Was that song on the radio that you knew every word in the lyric so many years ago? Do you struggle when someone asks you how old you are because you genuinely cannot remember?

The spiritual coaching and readings I do daily made it apparent that an easy-to-read and slightly interactive book was required. The book is for anyone who likes quiet time to read and reflect, deciding what is best for them. Most importantly, this book is aimed at you and making the best of you within your daily life. Sometimes good is good enough, and everything doesn't have to be perfect; loving yourself, being confident, and, most importantly, being happy are what matters. This book aims to help you design and live the life you want, even rekindle some of those forgotten dreams or create fabulous new ones.

The choice of chapters reflects the real-life assistance I have provided within coaching sessions, and it has been a delight to help people. Throughout the book, there are little exercises to help with your thinking. Rituals and meditations are included to help with your inner balance and spiritual strength. Try to do them each day, and they will make a difference to you.

Take ownership of your life, and how you make the best of it is your decision. Do not be put off by some of the stressful situations or awkward dynamics you encounter that may disrupt your progress. We all experience difficulties when we ask ourselves those deep questions, especially if they have been buried for a long time or we have been told to think or act in a certain way. Believe in yourself and embrace the vibrancy and colour of life.

Enjoy

Liz

INTRODUCTION

'Why bother'? That is an excellent question that most people ask themselves daily. Do you ask yourself that more than once a day? Or is it 'What is the point'? I will demonstrate many options for bringing colour to your monochrome days in this book. As the colour seeps in, you will feel vibrant and energised, exploring and seeing things you may never have believed previously about yourself. Some aspects will force you to question why you have done things in a certain way for so long, which may prove challenging. Try not to dwell on it or let it foster negative thoughts; keep progressing forward, enjoying every moment.

This book is about Your loneliness, your happiness, and the simple things you can do to engage with the spiritual world around you. Completing the challenges and exercises will affect how you feel about yourself. It is a gentle unfolding and awakening so that you start to feel comfortable exploring new things, unlike those fabulous New Year resolutions, which last all three, possibly four weeks. These are realistic ways in which some of your concerns and worries can engaged with and approached entirely differently.

The chapters unfold to bring together some ideas from personal coaching, a lot of spiritual awareness, and just a hint of magic and ritual; this book sets out to give you ideas to be inspirational in your life. If you want to unleash your inner God or Goddess, read on. Throw away that dowdy and humble approach you may have adopted for a long time and change to walking forward with your head held high, feeling fabulous. There is no preaching or banging a drum about what you should be doing. It opens the door to things that will feel natural, just like coming home to the authentic you.

This book is easy to read and has no long, arduous chapters, with gentle meditations and rituals to help you engage and connect with the world. It will help you embrace the problematic areas within many of your lives, such as how you feel about yourself. We are all different and experience Issues with money and love or the gut-wrenching disappointments in things or people we carry as baggage daily.

Push open the gate and start at a brilliant place, you.

CHAPTER 1

Who are you?

'Sometimes the lesson is to choose you.'

'Who am I'? It is a difficult question, and most of us put it to the back of the cupboard or lock it away in the draw. We do not want to know or believe that asking the question will reveal all the perceived bad things about ourselves. We forget that knowing ourselves and understanding more about what causes the reactions or fears within us helps us on our journey through life. Even a little self-knowledge will unlock your identity, allowing you to embrace the day confidently. You can put down building blocks of how you want your life to be and, importantly, who will share your life with you, not just a partner but friends, colleagues, and even your pets.

How do you describe yourself: wife, mother, partner, free spirit, or I am just ordinary? When you dig deep inside yourself, do you think the answer would be the same? Compared to the outer Persona, your inner Persona is rarely the same, and the desired description you would like to write could be different again. Please take a few moments over an indulgent coffee or whatever you drink, and try to work out who you are and compare it to the image you are frequently projecting.

A challenging thought is, what would you like your obituary to say? If someone is talking at your funeral, what would you like them to say about you? Most of us do not want to think about death but shift this to be a positive. Would people miss your smile? Or it's a shame no one will take me to the shops on Friday! If the latter, are you there for someone else's convenience, and it infringes on your time when you could be doing something for yourself?

Understanding what makes you happy will allow you to express what you want. Do you know you want to do something but are still determining what or how to do it or if it is what you want to do? Then you give up because it is all too difficult?

The answer is yes because you have never worked out or been brave enough to articulate what will make you happy. Try saying, 'I would love to go to the seaside and get an ice cream,' or some hidden desire you keep locked away. It is empowering, and you will feel much more positive if you allow it to come out. Stop being frightened about what others will say or think and say aloud what you want.

Your decision-making capability will be improved, allowing you to make the right choices for you, but only if you keep making decisions you believe in and truly desire. Your ability to say no when you do not want to do something as opposed to saying 'yes' and deeply regretting or resenting doing the chore or whatever it is. The stress this type of internal battle causes is vast and builds up over time into a real anxiety problem that will take a great deal of time and effort to heal. Weak decision-making influences many aspects of what you do: who you choose as a partner, what job to accept, or where to live. These all stem from not recognising and knowing who you are or what you want. So many of us have faced the consequence of poor decision-making and its significant impact on our lives when we get it wrong or go with the flow to keep the peace.

Unpicking a lousy choice or poorly made decision takes time and energy, and often, a significant upset forces that situation to be rectified. Then, there is dealing with the fallout of making such a change.

Understanding your self-control is an integral part of who you are. It will enable you to resist addictions, which can be drinking, drugs, or toxic people that drain you. Allowing yourself to be grounded (more about this later) and resolute in your decisions gives you a fantastic feeling of stability, knowing you will not be forced into anything you do not want to do.

Listing your passions and hobbies you either do or want to participate in is a great way to make a start. Choosing is always unique to you, and keep it personal. Sometimes, when we share information with friends, and it is not their passion, they can try to dissuade you. For example, if you have always wanted to walk across Australia and your best friend hates walking. Is it interest, or will it satisfy that urge to do something that makes you feel vital and energised? When you decided on your career, employed or self-employed, was it about something you loved, or did it just come along? Did you set yourself personal goals, such as doing that job for three years and doing something completely different? Was it because you were good at it or suited your introverted or extroverted personality type?

'There is no success without happiness'.

There are far too many questions, but they are the things that you need to ask yourself frequently. To fully function as the vibrant and beautiful person you are, you must have a profound grasp on who you are and where you fit in this world. No one is flawless, so accept you are imperfect and do not let it hold you back.

Be honest with yourself and keep challenging or pushing yourself forward. Never forget you have an inner voice (intuition) or gut feeling that will keep you out of trouble; remember to listen to it.

Exercise

Take pen and paper, not a laptop or phone. Write down three things that make you happy or that you have a passion to do. Then, write down three things that are stopping you from doing this. Pause, take a break, and then work out how you will do them and overcome the negative barriers. Keep the critical points visible at home to maintain your determination to achieve these goals. Reflect on them in 5 days and see if they are what you want; if not, repeat the process until you are delighted.

CHAPTER 2

Loving You

'Get Self-interested. It is not selfish.

Loving yourself sounds like an extraordinary concept. The thought of walking around saying, 'I love me' recalls arrogance, selfishness, and a heap of negative beliefs. Like some TV celebrities who enjoy being worshipped and believe they are Gods or Goddesses that no one can touch. It is nothing like that at all, so get rid of the stereotype.

What is Self-Love, and why do we ignore it?

Loving yourself is the best thing you can ever do for you. Being in love with all you are gives you self-confidence and enhances all aspects of your daily life. You will go to work with a spring in your step, smile at people confidently, and take all the daily challenges in your stride. Sounds good?

Then there must be a good reason why you do not do it.

What do we do?

Dislike what we see in the mirror each morning, peer at ourselves, looking for the wrinkle or the spot, even the grey hair. Then, agonise most of the day that everyone is looking at that spot. They do not care as they are worrying about their fat knees!

We constantly criticise ourselves for being fat, thin, and dull. Once we start, the list is endless, and we invest in a whole heap of diets and fads that achieve nothing but deplete the bank account. That gives you a whole new thing to be concerned about money!

Do you constantly feel someone is talking about you? So, you wonder about little conversations, even when you go for a coffee, assuming people are talking about you. Or believe anyone you encounter has an agenda, and you wonder why they asked that. When you walk into a room, and people look up, do you automatically assume they think negatively about you, so you fiddle with your skirt or hair?

An important one is carrying negative emotions from previous relationships and believing all future ones will be the same. You may have been hurt, cheated on, or lied to. A couple of days into a new relationship, your fingers are itching to check his/her phone, constantly asking them where they were or who they were with. Not only is this exhausting, but it guarantees that the relationship will not last. Then you are back, doubting that anyone will ever love you. Well, you caused that problem; face up to it.

Are you envious of others who have a seemingly perfect life? If I had a car like that or could afford those shoes, my life would be happier, excellent, or fulfilling. They may have a perfect life, which comes with understanding who they are and how to love themselves. Or are you seeing a veneer and have no idea what happens behind the scenes or the agonies they go through each morning looking in the mirror?

A big problem is that many people take every single comment to heart and think the worst. You are constantly repeating things to friends, asking what this comment meant. 'At work, somebody said to me. What do you think?' this type of thing will wake you up at 3 a.m. and plague you with self-doubt. The brevity of some text messages aids means you can interpret the message negatively. You text for hours until the other person gives up or blocks you. Then you shut yourself in your cave, nervous about going out, believing everyone is talking about you again!

Why do we do this?

Often, it is the belief that we should think of others and not ourselves, so we feel guilty about doing anything for ourselves. We carry the guilt of spending money on a fabulous treat, even a bar of chocolate, sneaking new shopping bags in, or agonising over a new bubble bath. Yet, have no worries about spending a fortune on someone else.

You cannot take a compliment such as someone liking your shoes, and you make the excuse of 'they were in the sale' or some deal, even found in a skip, instead of smiling and saying, 'Thank you, I love them.'

It is so easy to hold and carry the spiteful look that someone gives us. Because the fundamental love for you is not there, it is pretty easy for this to dive into a tailspin of depression or knee-jerk responses. Once that downward spiral starts, stopping and pulling yourself back out of it isn't easy.

To love yourself is to come to terms with those aspects of you that cannot be changed. You need to build:

- Your self-respect and self-esteem
- A positive self-image
- Unconditional self-acceptance

What do these look like within our daily lives, and where do you start?

- Accepting yourself for who and what you are
- Care as much about you as you do about others.
- Unconditionally accept that you may have flaws – so what? All of them are the real you – love it, embrace it, and do not apologise!
- Maintain your boundaries, and do not give in to pressure!
- Do NOT hate what you see in the mirror!
- Be authentic; remember to speak your truth.
- Forgive yourself; we all do stupid things, and move on.

That is a straightforward list to read and a difficult one to achieve. Years of conditioning holding you back, even peer group pressure wanting to maintain you in a place that suits them all, put shackles on us. Even saying something affirming and upbeat can feel clumsy or awkward at first. Keep doing this, and the words will soon start to flow naturally. Enjoy putting some colour or humour into your affirmations. By the end of this book, you will be loving yourself and delighting in saying or chanting your morning's unique words. Or to take from Tarot, 'I am the Empress; I have got this.'

Exercise

Affirmations are a fabulous way to feel positive about yourself. Take time to write a couple and say them out loud every morning when you get up. Please make sure they are relevant to how you feel about you. Over time, these will change, so be sure to update and modify depending on your thoughts. Here are some suggestions:

'I radiate self-love and have a right to be happy.'

'I am worthy of achieving my needs and desires.'

Look in the mirror each morning, and instead of seeing something negative, see the fantastic, beautiful, and vibrant person you are.

Ritual for Self-Love

Making time for a ritual that will help you love your body and everything about you should be a significant component of your belief structure. Saying an Affirmation or Mantra is brilliant, but not if you do not believe what you say every time you look in the mirror. Taking time to know you and your body and indulging in it will help build your confidence, and it does not have to cost much money.

Potions

Making a potion especially for you is deeply satisfying. Aromatherapy balms, body lotions, or oils are freely available, but adding ingredients that make them unique demonstrates that you can give time over to yourself—knowing the smells or textures you enjoy. Experiment with them and mix blends.

Use Vanilla oil as it promotes wellbeing and sensuality. Jasmine Flower extracts are stress-releasing and alleviate low self-esteem.

Take time to soak in a bath with some lovely bath oil to help you relax. Use your potion as a body rub and ensure that as you massage it, you say how wonderful you are—even adding essential oil to your water. Use a body scrub and pay attention to elbows and knees areas that can hold negativity spiritually.

Make yourself a special drink, such as water with lemon balm. This combination is strongly associated with the Moon and the Goddess Diana. You can add vanilla and make a warming drink to calm you and restore the feelings of self-love.

Some crave a hot chocolate or another indulgence; keep this as a special treat and not part of a ritual. Once a practice becomes a habit, you are more likely to do it. Put in your diary time for your 'Me time.' Develop your own and enjoy taking the time to research things that stimulate your senses and add to your feelings of self-worth.

Cleansing and releasing all the negative feelings you have kept locked away for many years is liberating—enabling you to forget personal judgemental thoughts about yourself, making you feel at peace. Your personality will gently change, which is the start of your healing time.

Repeat these rituals regularly until they become part of your routine, and combined with the positive affirmations, they will make a difference in your journey to discover the authentic you.

CHAPTER 3

The Confident You

'Remember, you are the most important person in the universe.'

Lack of confidence is a massive problem for many people. It can range from a minor lack of belief that they cannot do something to massive self-worth and self-esteem issues. Feeling this way will make you isolated and lack connection with people. Then, your ability to engage with daily life will be negatively impacted and lead to several confidence issues. That is a broad term and is unique to all of us. Do you try four outfits before you go out and convince yourself there is nothing in your wardrobe you could wear?

In turn, it makes you feel more and more unworthy. You may think you are searching for something but are unsure what. Or making yourself the person you think other people would like you to be? Just reading about it is exhausting, so how must it feel to live it? All this agonising constantly takes you away from the real you, and then you slip into a downward spiral that may result in some actual mental health or anxiety problems.

Life can be lonely, even if many friends and family surround you. The experience of that hollow pang inside you and the question is this is as good as it gets? Often, people feel that I am not sure I am from this planet, so why am I here? Or do you spend time waiting for that special something or someone to turn up and constantly end up disappointed? Then, it is time for compensation tactics to kick in, like addictions such as drinking, eating, or shopping, but in the longer term, they do not help at all and typically add to the cycle of you not loving yourself enough.

Getting rid of self-limiting beliefs is an excellent way to start, as well as recognising those ideals that you believe govern you are not cast in stone and can be changed. That was easy to read and far harder to achieve. Choose to do things with like-minded people and watch your world change. Frequently referred to in the spiritual world as 'Know your tribe and dance with them.' The moral of this is do not pretend to be someone you are not; the energy of keeping this facade is exhausting and filled with rejection.

Why does Self-confidence matter?

It is vital in every aspect of our lives. Many people struggle to find their confidence and maintain it when there is the humdrum of a busy life. One slip and it is all forgotten, and the cycle begins again. It needs to become part of your DNA and is there without you realising it. There may be one area where you are strong and confident, which is never a problem, but other aspects of your life terrify you. For example, can you make decisions at work, manage a team, deliver a project on time, or succeed at sales? Yet if you are asked about a social situation, does it cause you significant problems, or when someone pays you a personal compliment, do you cringe?

People without self-confidence are less likely to achieve the success they would hope for. Compounding negative emotions directed towards you, such as a simple barbed comment, hurts you. This build-up of contained negativity will grow and can escalate quickly. Your low confidence levels will start to manifest in fear of the unknown or make you constantly unhappy about your appearance. Or your ability to interact socially. How cruel is that inner self? 'Well, you are just fat, dumb, or unhappy; no one would want you at the party!'

A big step on the positive path is understanding and trusting your judgment so that you are at ease with the real you. Please feel free to rigidly measure like analytical statistics or a scientific rule easily put into a formula. You will feel buoyant and confident some days, but others will be down days. If you understand that cycle, such as you may change or be in synchronicity with the moon phases, then that is positive because you can compensate. If the emotions are more extended and profound, you need to do something about it. That can be seeking real help or taking the time to meditate and come to explore those more profound parts of you that need to open and understand. Develop a spiritual practice, or give yourself a fabulous treat.

As a warning, confidence is also a problem as it makes you believe you can do anything and will come across as arrogant. Then, people delight in your failure. Sometimes, you will be 'faking it' or saying today, I will be confident and bullishly barging your way through the day.

Let us Analyse Confidence.

'Self-esteem is what we think and feel and believe about ourselves. Self-worth is recognising that.'

Dr Christina Hibbert

Ask yourself if you feel unworthy of the respect of others, including being loved by others, family, friends, or relationships. Your negative thoughts tend to creep into your unconscious mind from comments and issues you have experienced, a barbed comment years ago that sticks. Sometimes, this is even just perceived behaviour, but it still has had an impact. This results in sad and destructive behaviour towards yourself. Resulting in bad feelings outwardly and inwardly. When you live in that low vibration, anything anyone says is negative. 'That is a great top you are wearing. Instead of thinking great, so pleased I chose it today, the negative thought process is 'What was wrong with the one I wore yesterday?' or 'It looks awful, and they are just being mean.'

Self-confidence is an attitude about your skills and abilities, knowing you can trust and control yourself. You have a good knowledge of your strengths and weaknesses and can maintain a positive perspective through whatever arises. Lacking that confidence means you will always underachieve, doubt your abilities, and feel paranoid about what other people think of you.

Self-esteem is about loving yourself, your thoughts and emotions, and your interactions with the world. You should feel good about yourself and see yourself as deserving the respect of others.

Self-worth is how good you feel about yourself, and when you do not have it, it fosters an innate sense of being let down or impacts your sense of dignity. It is the value that you place on your achievements.

Greater self-confidence gives you freedom from self-doubt and negative thoughts about you and everything you do. You can take more intelligent risks and happily move outside your comfort zone.

Self Esteem

Many things cause low self-esteem. Frequently, it is the build-up of several factors that contrive to make you feel bad. Such as childhood problems, stress in life, relationship breakdowns, financial problems, and anything else you tend to put into the mix.

Signs of low Self-Esteem

- Difficulty speaking and prioritising your own needs
- Always saying 'I am sorry' for everyday actions
- You never rock the boat and frequently keep your head down
- Do not feel deserving of anything good or praise
- You struggle to make decisions
- You do not have any boundaries
- Doing things such as constantly buying gifts or being excessively generous to people
- Negative thoughts about you and everything you do

Low self-esteem is not a character trait and certainly is not humility. The inability to speak out in meetings and threats such as relationship problems are incredibly damaging.

Recognising that you have some of these traits is a brilliant start to recognising problem areas and moving towards recognising how precious you are.

Build your self-confidence!

- Do something positive, such as get help, start reading up to understand the origins of this within you, and be honest with yourself.
- Understand the things you enjoy and do them.
- Prioritise your goals and avoid being derailed by others' demands and requests when the guilt kicks in and you prioritise them.
- Pause and reflect before saying 'yes' to anything. Ask yourself if you want to do it. If you do not say so in a polite but firm way
- Lift yourself 'I am beautiful,' 'I am confident,' I am worthy.'
- Meditation and positive affirmations do work; keep doing them
- Notice when you start to compare yourself to others. Positively limit this behaviour.

- Find a favourite way to relax and pamper yourself.
- STOP saying, 'I am sorry,' and try alternatives such as 'Excuse me' or 'Thank you for your patience/understanding.'
- Develop a personal brand/image that will set you apart from the crowd and reflect who you are, such as the type of jewellery you wear and different colours, even if you can match them to the chakra colours. If you feel low energy, wear the vibrant orange of the sacral chakra and see how it makes you smile.
- Take a different route to the shops, or avoid walking/driving the same way when you are out. Even have a spontaneous adventure involving travel.
- Be brave to join an interest group with people you do not know. Adopting this approach is a clean slate, so go in as you and love it.

Confidence in the Business World

Many of us have a business or are hoping to start one. Anything new can bring many challenges or insecurities into daily decisions. Several patterns have emerged from the coaching and spiritual therapy sessions I have conducted, reflecting problems in people's business-led confidence. Even if you have a long-term employed career, a crisis of confidence will impact you at some stage in your life. Suddenly, you get a boss that you cannot get along with. You are rejected for promotion, or even you are ignored during meetings. You constantly fear redundancy or have experienced some workplace abuse or bullying. Perhaps you said or did something others call a 'stupid decision,' you feel this is now your brand.

Confidence within your working environment can adopt all the good things suggested, but, in some cases, you may need to go a step further. Sadly, how we are perceived at work directly impacts our ability to get pay raises and promotions. When you seem invisible, it severely impacts your confidence to do things and makes you fearful of the next time you get a review or even when someone new joins the business. There are some easy things you can do that will help you.

- Pay attention to the way you want to look. Do not feel you have to conform, but if you like the relaxed approach, loose hair, or tee-shirt, adopt it, but always ensure your hair is clean. The grooming issues are about personal self-respect and give the impression that you care about yourself so that you will care about your job. Forgetting personal hygiene is sometimes seen as an early step to forms of health issues.

- Think positively in everything you do. Even if you disagree, say 'Interesting concept' or 'I like your perspective' and firmly and persuasively put your point across
- Listen to your thoughts and understand your limitations – such as not volunteering for everything or something entirely outside your capability and rapidly regret it.
- Put your positive thoughts into action.
- Be kind. Being a good person is positive. Know you are kind, but remember there is no need to be overly generous and feel guilty when you cannot fulfil it.
- Making a good first impression is essential; people remember it
- Maintain eye contact and do not fidget during an interview or meeting.
- Adopt an open posture and empty your hands, indicating a desire to communicate.
- Introduce yourself to someone new and articulate what you do with a smile, not fiddling with your earrings or watch

- Volunteer to give a speech or presentation about something you are passionate about

'One important key to success is self-confidence
A key to self-confidence is preparation.'

Arthur Ashe

How do you prepare for self-confidence?

It sounds bizarre that you consciously need to prepare to be self-confident. By undertaking some simple tasks and achieving them, you will build your strength and faith in yourself to take on much more significant challenges. We have spent a lot of time discussing confidence and suggestions you can take forward. Not all will apply to you, but even adopting a few will make a big difference to all aspects of your life.

- Always be prepared. Do the planning for a meeting, talk, or journey unless you are a free spirit and just like to jump in the car and disappear.
- Understand what your principles are and stick to them

- Speak calmly and slowly, and this shows you are confident in what you are saying and want to deliver it well
- Stand tall. No hunching in the corner or hiding behind your computer; you can give an outstanding and dazzling smile. It will make you feel better
- Set a small goal and achieve it, then look to the next one
- Be grateful, give thanks for everything, even the bad things, say 'I give gratitude for this lesson' and believe it and mean it
- De-clutter makes you feel more in control.

Accepting yourself and taking care of who you are is critical to being the authentic you. You want to be a person who feels worthy and not the one who is always on the back foot, watching where the next problem or issue will come from and make you feel bad again.

Trying new things, a new hobby, or looking at things from a different perspective are always great ways to build belief in yourself. If it is body image, do you hate the way you look, or is it peer pressure that has made you feel like that? If it is peer pressure, try being the real you.

If you do not want to diet, change your clothes and try wearing them differently. A good scarf will hide plenty; if it is a bright colour, it will make you feel vibrant. If you feel lonely and isolated, try a new sort of club or begin to develop your spirituality. Every small step is a significant victory.

There are significant benefits to high self-esteem

- You are more assertive in expressing your needs and opinions
- You are confident in your ability to make decisions and stick to them
- You can build and maintain secure relationships
- You are less critical of yourself and have realistic expectations

Exercise

Think about a situation that has stayed with you from a work or school perspective. What is it? Write it in your journal or workbook and reflect on that situation. Would you have handled it differently? Now that there is distance between the event/situation, was it wrong? Write to forgive yourself and the others, give thanks for the lesson, and move on.

CHAPTER 4

Spiritual Confidence

Later, we cover more about your spiritual connection and how that enhances all you do— not forgetting a bit of magic you can weave into your life.

Spiritual confidence is about knowing without understanding how you learn. That may sound complicated, but you will have heard of gut feeling or intuition. It is the inner voice that you should trust but, most of the time, frequently dismiss. How many people say, 'It was lucky I did not get on that bus as it crashed' or some other type of story? That is an extreme example.

When you have the absolute conviction to free your soul and destroy all doubts and fears, your heart will be filled with love. You will cease to be dependent on external influences or crutches. As incredible as it sounds, it is achievable. You need to believe and put some positive work into your mindset to get there.

Not having enough money is always seen as a sign of unworthiness. This vibration can translate into 'I am unable to receive' or fail at attempts to attract money. As a result, you ping-pong through life. My pay rise was low, and I am not worthy, so I cannot receive the bonus/increased amount, and you start to spiral downwards, which impacts the quality of your work. Next year, there will be no pay rise again! It would be best to shift your vibration onto receive mode and, as part of your affirmations, 'I give thanks for the lessons and gifts in abundance.' Let the universe know you are ready to have blessings bestowed upon you.

In many articles that advise who you need to be, the foundation is that you are flawed somehow. You are fat, and you do not know how to connect with people; this is what you should eat, etc. True fulfilment comes when you awaken your inner purpose, and life becomes rich beyond measure. Most importantly, you achieve inner peace, which we all crave. To breathe and feel warm and comfortable without stress or anxiety.

How do you get spiritually aware? You need to know who you are and then move the ego from your spirit. Everyone, including you, is perfect, but surrounding them is a web of illusion and false desires or beliefs, and this web has become a prison. A prison that you must work hard to keep pace with as delusions only grow. Trying to do this is exhausting, and only some people can continue doing this for extended periods without causing health and wellbeing problems.

Once you recall who you are and become aware of your inner spirit, achieving the rest is much easier. Living in spiritual awareness is knowing you are perfect and have peace. If you are unhappy, then you are being guided by your ego.

All the other things we have covered still apply, but these are simple guidance tools to help you overcome your inner fears.

- Tame your mind, and this is when you make the unconscious thoughts and desires of what you want to achieve into the forefront of your conscious mind. A simple way is to keep a journal or scrapbook. If it is a new job/house or something you have feared doing, write it down, believe in it, and add to the information so you are confident that you can move forward with it. Sometimes, this is called a vision board; you can put it up in your kitchen or in a visible position. Whatever method works for you, try it.

- Believe in unconditional love. Please eliminate hateful and judgemental thoughts, as they fill you with negativity. If someone says something spiteful, ignore it. They have thrown mud at you, and it will stick to them.
- Meditation is difficult if you have never done this before, and there is a section on successful meditation. Take a short time of complete peace to concentrate on your breathing and feel whole. The skill is relaxing and giving yourself the quiet and space to do this.
- Develop and understand mindfulness; make it part of your routine and your approach to life.

Negative comments are so destructive that once you have accepted them, they stick, and it is tough to get away from their long and powerful tentacles. Work out how to deal with negative comments and criticism and turn them into positives.

- Know your strengths and weaknesses and be confident in them
- Acknowledge we all make mistakes; they are learning opportunities
- Accept compliments and compliment yourself – even ask for details. Same with criticism, take the comments boldly
- Criticism is a learning experience; everyone perceives the world differently. It is just someone else's opinion, and do not be defensive. Listen to what is said, and do not make your reality around it
- Be generally cheerful and have a positive outlook on life

Fearing rejection, abandonment, or even lack of approval stems from our lack of belief in ourselves. It would be best if you had help and connection. That robust and grounded core has crumbled slightly, and nothing feels stable.

Dig out what is repressed within you and give yourself permission to rediscover and redevelop what is the real you. Aid yourself with mantras that are positive, uplifting, and the complete opposite of what you would typically write.

Replace all that people-pleasing and care for the real you. Doing this type of work will take time, as you have probably neglected yourself for a long time. Every time you do something for someone else, do something for yourself, even if it is just a cuppa. That exchange, often called energy exchange, is vital in the spiritual world, but respect exchange is the same. It does not have to be about money. It can be something tiny, such as a toffee. Praise yourself, and this is my treat. Thank you.

Exercise

List three times when you have heard that inner voice and ignored it. Looking back, what would have been different? How will you regard it in the future?

CHAPTER 5

How do you Communicate?

Effective communication is often a massive problem in our world now. Even talking with your family is complex; age differences cause a lack of understanding of terminology. Far too many buzzwords or abbreviations do not easily bridge the age gaps. Clear speech is essential, but how you express yourself and knowing the impact your words are having is a crucial part of your development.

Sometimes, you need to speak about what you want. Hearing out loud makes it seem real, achievable, or absolutely the wrong thing to do! When you write an affirmation and speak it – suddenly it is feasible: 'I am beautiful and vibrant.' There you have said it.

You may decide to change it, or it will require updating; keep adding to what you want. 'I am me, beautiful and confident' – see the subtle change and make sure the slight difference reflects what you want.

Speaking out loud is also a way of dredging a solution from the deepest recesses of your brain. I am not suggesting you chat away to yourself on the train, but maybe out in nature. Speak your challenge to the universe. It is amazing how your subconscious mind finds a solution or provides you with a new path.

If you must give information to people, work out how they like to receive it. Are you giving it in the correct way that suits them? Otherwise, it will not make any difference; they cannot hear it.

Without going into detail about how people often like to work with information such as auditory – you need to hear it. Tell people succinctly and describe what you are saying. Talk to friends about what you want to achieve, and speaking makes it real. Part of what we will cover is raising your vibration; speaking these to the universe or just when you are in the bath will make them tangible and attainable.

Visual plans in front of you make more sense to some people or draw a mind map. Often, a group of people will discuss ideas, but immediately, they are put into a visual form. So, if you are explaining something or want to gain support for what you are doing, consider what your audience will like or like. If you adopt a method that does not resonate with them, they will look away or get bored. Seeing this reaction diminishes your confidence.

- Mind maps are good for showing the links between several ideas—and the creative pathways of your thinking. The finished item will give you a complete overview and an image you can put on the wall.
- Rich Text is a picture of your journey to achieve what you want and the outcome. So, if it is the tea shop, the start may be the estate agent, moving on to choosing the décor and what you will sell all in pictures. Then, the final, the shop's interior or the outside signage, not forgetting people inside enjoying themselves.
- Others prefer a simplified project plan of what, how, and timescales. Or a SWOT (Strengths, Weaknesses, Opportunities, and Threats) analysis. The analytical comparisons are what they understand.

Find out what is best for you and use the tool. The planning and detail are inspiring, and they help you focus on your end goal. Remember to include the challenges, the competition, or anything you feel may be a blocker.

Communications barriers

- Non-verbal facial expressions, hand gestures, eye contact, and posture are the things to notice and what people see about you.
- Language! Too technical, abusive, indulgence in words
- Ambiguity: no idea what the actual message is or why it is being said
- Overload – speaking too long and leading to receiver exhaustion and boredom.
- Attitudes – Fixed views from some people and saying something that encourages them to be disruptive
- Age/gender – the type of language that is adopted. Some age groups have no idea what is being said.
- Jumping to conclusions – Pick one aspect and ignore everything else.

Exercise

Pick three friends, colleagues, or family members and write a plan for how you would communicate with them about your newfound self-confidence. Consider they may not be comfortable with the 'new' you, so you have to be able to show them this is who you are.

CHAPTER 6

Spiritual Communications

The spiritual laws of communication are the fundamental and universal principles upon which happy and healthy communications are based. What does this mean? The growing understanding and respect of all things spiritual is vital to ensuring we have harmony in our lives. Broadening this to what we say and do directly impacts what and how we communicate. Spiritual does not mean you must be religious to understand where you are within the great cycle of nature and the universe. Respecting that will enable more effective language and communications. Strangely, this will make you feel so much better about yourself when you can see your words positively impact others, even if you are delivering not such good news.

- Communicate from the heart, do not see anger in others but see their confusion and insecurity, and that is what is driving them to speak out in such a forceful way.
- Look at the potential in everything; it will open the way you communicate and put a positive slant. Everything is about a lesson and growth.
- Soften how you speak and articulate your words with compassion, not bitterness or vitriol. All this does is increase your levels of stress.
- Show some humility. Please do not feel this is about being weak or giving in.
- Do not embellish or exaggerate 'Your always' or 'You never'; it is artificial for effect.
- Accept that things are not perfect; we all stumble, so there are many people you will never agree with. Recognise in yourself that you make mistakes. Please do not dwell on them or keep raising them. Frequently, it makes you feel worse, not better.

Communicate with spirit or your soul.

The conversations you have with your soul or spirit guide shape a great deal of your decision-making. If you ignore the inner voice and bulldoze your way through life, you are missing guidance from your internal and authentic self.

Our souls communicate differently through feelings, intuition, and symbols. So, we frequently ignore or mistrust these.

- Everyone has that inner voice, a fantastic way to establish your life purpose. Listen to it, and the messages will amaze you.
- Pay attention to your dreams, the symbols, and the story
- Notice repetitive words and numbers 11:11 or 2020! It is a wake-up, so ask yourself what the meaning and hidden message are.
- Animal omens and guides. Trust your gut and how you respond when you see a magpie or black cat. Are they good or bad? Several noisy crows you see daily tell you to calm your inner agitation.
- Synchronicity or serendipity. Synchronicities are about moments of meaningful coincidence where worlds align. Serendipity is about a happy accident or a meeting of chance – finding money is a coat pocket.
- Gut feeling is an unexplainable sensation that tells you to do or not to do something. Usually referred to as intuition or the inner

voice. We all have it, trust it. There is a book by Malcolm Gladwell called 'Blink' that states that the first impression you have of something is usually the correct one.

CHAPTER 7

Walking with Your Shadow

What is our Inner Shadow?

Hearing the word Shadow for the first time can be pretty disturbing. Fearing that you may have something lurking within you over which you have no control that could pop out at any moment, just like in the film Alien. Or, more importantly, do not believe it applies to you and deny you have any inner secrets or things tucked away, never to be revealed.

A shadow is a negative, like when you walk in the sunshine and see your own Shadow. The Shadow within is often an automatic and even unintentional response to events or people even situations. This reaction, which emanates from your unconscious, can often take you by surprise and leave you bewildered. Sometimes, this is referred to as a knee-jerk reaction. You may act defensively or dig your heels in to resist change or show some aggressive behaviour. People around you may mutter that this is entirely out of character, but you have put a blot on what you want to achieve or how they feel about you.

This Shadow is a part of you and not a negative in the detrimental sense. The shadow side of your personality is the part you often do not want to admit to and do everything to suppress it or keep it locked in an inner box. You are constantly hoping that the key has been thrown away. You often have no control until something happens; it flies out again, and the words or actions are out before you realise it!

Why do you need to look at your own Shadow? By taking time to appreciate, review, and understand all your emotions, your life will be far more fulfilling. It is a way of achieving emotional freedom and living more authentically. When correctly channelled, your Shadow has traits you can use wisely to further your personal development. The hidden friend.

Accepting a deeply hidden secret, behaviour, or part of you that needs healing is the only way to self-love. You cannot say you love yourself completely, but not that bit! Discarding critical aspects of who you are always means you are not whole or holistically balanced.

The shadow part of us can create blockages and cause harm within our lives as it prevents all attempts to work for the greater good, especially as we have made significant steps towards building our confidence.

Where does this come from?

Carl Jung conceived the shadow self and used the word Shadow to refer to the hidden parts of our being. Working on your sunny side is easy, and you feel great at a superficial level. Hair glossy, great shoes beaming smile, but this surface illusion is not transforming your inner core.

Jung believed that the more the Shadow is ignored, the more it will sabotage your life.

His Archetypes

- The Self
- The Persona
- The Shadow
- The Anima/Animus

In my courses, we have worked with some of these previously.

By integrating the Shadow, our lives become more balanced, and we can live comfortably and emotionally fulfilled.

'Until you make the unconscious conscious, it will direct your life.

And you will call it fate' Carl Jung

It is tough to recognise this behaviour significantly if you have repressed parts of yourself for a long time. At some point in life, you discover pain and quickly start to suppress it. Parental behaviour, bullying, abuse, and even seeing someone misbehave with an animal. Conditioning by parents or a forceful partner. Everyone will have their suffering, which was then quickly contained and repressed.

Classic signs that indicate a lurking shadow are anger, blame, laziness, insecurity, and jealousy. These are signs of internal pain that are genuine and unique to you. The Persona is the loveable self, and the Shadow is the face we hide.

What is dealing with your Shadow?

The constant use of the word Shadow may cause you to react. Good! Just like when you walk in the sunshine, your Shadow is attached to you somewhere, and so is your inner one.

Skeletons in the cupboard, inner demons; we all have them and do not want to talk about them or face up to them. How many celebrities hate it when their skeletons or hidden secrets are revealed? There would be no news story if they just laughed it off. When we look radiant, the darkness within seems more apparent when we enjoy ourselves. You will never find true happiness and peace if you allow that to control you. How you will feel is low self-worth, addictions, or constant health issues.

Everything talked about so far can easily clog up your mind, and you start not to think clearly about situations. It is you who must face up to your pain and not keep locking it away or running away from it.

WHY?

- There will be a significant improvement in your relationships, all of them, through

understanding yourself and how you accept others.
- Your energy levels will increase, and your immune system will be boosted. No longer will you be using up all that energy suppressing things?
- Overall, your sense of wellbeing and general mood will improve
- Your ability to communicate effectively with others will be better, knowing how to say things in the most appropriate way
- You are going to be able to set boundaries, your own, so no longer can people encroach, and you will understand and respect the boundaries of others
- It will stop your cycle of digging big holes and falling into them!
- You will be grounded and balanced, and your ability to perceive will be much more evident.

Suppose you think of Dr. Jekyll and Mr Hyde, the great novel. Dr Jekyll could not control the actions of his darker half. When you deny qualities in yourself, you see it in others.

For example, if you get irritated when someone is rude, you may need to face up to your rudeness and behaviours.

Where to start

Before going any further, you must reflect/ meditate and be honest with yourself. Are you struggling with low self-esteem or lack of self-love? If so, please re-read those chapters. Any other work now will be too complex, and you need to build up your personal belief in yourself. It can be disturbing to open yourself up to you, so take the opportunity to develop some spiritual strength and gain emotional strength to aid you in working through this.

Self-love starts here. It would help if you made the time to do it and not approach it half-heartedly. We keep repeating about self-love as this is the foundation stone to build the future you in glorious technicolour.

It would help if you opened that storage box to progress your journey and move through that tremendously significant gateway to a more fulfilling life. If you are saying:

'I am not like that.'

'I have never cheated/stolen'

'I should always be receiving praise as I am so good at what I do.'

It is time to progress. The shadow side is often created in childhood as part of natural ego or conditioning. If your parents were clear about good and bad, you may constantly have sought their approval to be 'good' and avoided anything unacceptable. This, in turn, may have stunted your emotional growth to fit in with family or school friends in which you developed the ability to behave in a certain way.

You may have been told showing any form of anger is terrible, so you repressed it instead of being taught acceptable ways of showing your emotion. At some stage in your life, that needs to go 'pop.' Otherwise, it will cause you endless problems, plus there is a type of relief in letting go, just like letting out a big sigh.

It may have been the same in school, adopting behaviours to avoid bullies and in relationships, being the person they want/ed you to be. Or constantly trying to gain the teacher's approval or recognition from your boss.

You now may find yourself demonstrating:

- Hypocrisy
- Lies
- Bursts of rage or anger
- Phobias
- Narcissism
- Greed and additions

Suppose you are brave enough to admit to them! Remaining ignorant and choosing to forget about the collection of disowned parts within you will only exponentially increase. You will demonstrate unacceptable behaviour without realising it. Say inappropriate things and can alienate someone very quickly. They are extremes, but many of us have that little demon that comes out when least expected.

Are you ready to progress?

It would be best to feel ready to confront your truth and be strong and confident enough to deal with it. Once you start on the progressive path, going backwards is not a great idea.

- Safe space: you need to create one as a place you can visit visually during meditation or even a corner of your home. The area is sacred, special, and unique to you.
- Be good to you. It is easy to say, but it is a challenging journey, and you need to understand and give yourself plenty of love, praise, and
- positive things.
- Could you write it down? This will help you learn, and in the writing process, you will gain clarity.

Some ideas of what to do

Everyone is unique and special so that the steps may differ, and you must work precisely with what is within your comfort zone.

- Daily, pay attention to your emotional reactions. What is making you feel powerful, angry, and distressed? Did you cry at a film or shout at the radio? Out of the emotions, what ranked the highest?
- Make sure you are open and observant, paying close attention to how you feel during that emotion.

- When thinking about the inner demons, try to recognise how long and where they have been hidden within your soul. Whatever comes out, please pay attention to it, as it is revealing parts of you that you may not ever think about.
- Start doing something, a project, or an ambition you have always wanted to achieve but avoided, like writing a book or creating a new part of the garden. As you finally begin something you inwardly have desired, note how you are feeling. Do not stop or restrain yourself; push on and give yourself little milestones if you believe it will motivate you more.
- Keep a record. Progress reports each week. I have achieved. If you slipped, note your comments and give yourself some insight as to why.
- Embrace the left and right paths. Traditionally, the left way has always been associated with the dark or radical side. The right hand is what we pursue positivity and connect with our higher. It would help if you embraced both to feel balanced.

The Shadow Traits

These are some examples of the traits a shadow side will appear. They may help you to understand some of your behaviours, as this is a critical step in integrating and working with them.

- Ego will show as pride, self-indulgence, and narcissism. This has a root cause of feeling that you are a nobody and not good enough for anyone.
- The root of this is a desire to regain control of everything.
- Untrustworthy, deceitful, or unreliable. The root of this is a general fear of life.
- Unstable, weepy, or overemotional. The root of this is a feeling that you are unlovable and powerless to resolve emotional pain.
- Controlling, bossy, or obsessive behaviour will come from mistrust in life and feelings of abandonment.
- Sarcastic, hostile, and even resentful mannerisms are adopted to alleviate feelings of vulnerability and the need to protect yourself.
- Sexual, sadistic, constantly desiring, and even vulgar stems from suppressed sexual energy or unresolved childhood wounds.

- Scared, timid, or weak. Coming from a refusal to grow up

These are just a few examples to give you an idea of what you must look for within yourself. To progress now, you will feel a little insecure as you deal with a significant part of yourself that has been hidden for a long time. It will also not be solved in an hour by a quick meditation, hot chocolate, and a bit of self-love! You are going to have to work hard at this.

Exercises to progress

Once again, only you can do this, which can be a slow process. The best place to start is with meditation and a plan. If you do not meditate, it is time to start, as it gives you a complete and quiet time to align yourself to begin.

Then, write a plan as part of your notebook of observations.

- Record and watch your reactions to things. The more you pay attention to the little mannerisms, the greater your chance of identifying yours increases. So, if you see someone getting very annoyed, watch the process and reflect on how you feel about it. Or if there is someone that irritates you, why?

- Talk to yourself, sometimes called the inner dialogue. Speak out loud about things that have happened in the day, especially if there is a sudden reaction. 'why did I shout at that person?' or 'Why did I cross the road when x was coming along?'.
- Challenge and list your positive qualities and what you believe is good about you. Then, list what the opposite is and if any of them identify with you.

The Process

Choose something you want to work with once you have taken the time to understand yourself.

Face it. Describe or talk, even draw what most upsets you—the thought of cheating, lies, or certain behaviours. Once again, this is unique and personal to you.

Talk to the behaviour and ask it questions

- Why are you doing this?
- What do you want?

- What is the lesson you are trying to show me?

Live it for a while

Take on the energies or the behaviours that fascinate you. If you are timid, typically change direction, or if you are always holding yourself back.

- Be angry at things.
- Express jealousy at objects or people
- Walk around declaring you are radiant and beautiful (you should be doing this anyway!)

Clarity of speech is not a suggestion that you get angry at people daily. Try them before your meditation session to assess when you are calm. In real life, be more assertive or proud of how you look.

Own It

Re-integrate that quality into your life, but not to the extent it becomes dominant. Set your boundaries, and walk with a spring in your step. Understand why you feel angry and only use it when you need that gravitas to how you speak.

At first, this may seem unclear, but if you have worked through where you believe your Shadow originated and how it manifests in your day-to-day life, this final step will make sense.

If you struggle with anger, you may take up some form of exercise, boxing, or yoga – depending on how you wish to re-integrate to become balanced.

- Use meditation or mindfulness to centre yourself.
- Cultivate an air of self-compassion and unconditional love for you and the process you are going through
- Start to generate greater self-awareness by writing, observing, and giving time to do this.
- Be honest about what suppressed or became a parked behaviour throughout your life.
- Open the inner box and confront your pain and fear. Draw it and release it
- Record constantly what you find and how you are feeling
- Work out how to integrate. You may need to get it out and remove it as it does not fit with who you are now.

Working with all these elements is a fascinating part of your journey, and this chapter has been covered in detail. Take time to read several times, as there is much information and work to do! Remember, if your self-esteem is low and you are feeling vulnerable, feel confident in the other chapters first before enjoying and being part of the magical whole of you.

CHAPTER 8

Meditation

The art and practice of meditating are a fantastic way of connecting with our inner self. It is a way of slowing down the pace and making the most of your energy, knowing how to breathe, and letting life flow past. Often, finding time without distraction is a problem. The temptation to keep your phone on is huge or allow your mind to wander, so you end up doing something else and not returning to what you set out to do. Guided meditations are a great help and cover a wide variety of things you wish to deal with. Follow them and be in the moment of what they are saying; try not to be second guessing what comes next.

Make the time to design your meditation and go to the core of what causes you problems, physical or mental. Pay particular attention to your environment and decide if there will be a focus point: a statue or a crystal. Even meditate about something you want to achieve and write it on paper as the focus point. The aim is to be happy and content in all that you do. Loving yourself, your body, and even the quirks of your personality that others may have made disparaging comments about.

So far in this book, we have covered many detailed topics about you. Now is the time to relax and start to reflect.

Meditation to Connect with your inner self

Allow yourself some time without distraction, and you must be comfortable. Sit on the floor or a comfy chair, use a cushion to support you and wear something that allows you freedom of movement.

Use music if you wish, but keep yourself from being distracted.

Feel relaxed within your environment and understand if you are new to meditation, you may only be able to do this for a short while. Do not push yourself.

Breathe deeply through the nose and maintain this deep and regular breathing. Be aware of the sounds of life-giving breath filling your body. Quiet and still your mind.

Please pay attention to your body and how it is feeling. Do you ache or have pangs or residual hurt from comments made to you? Send the warmth to that place and feel it at ease.

Hold a crystal or object that you care about and will bring you strength

As you breathe, think, 'I am worthy; I am enough.'

'I am worthy of love, and all fear is banished.'

'My heart is filled with joy'

Let the warmth permeate your body, and enjoy the moment of love and peace.

Take some more breaths and softly open your eyes.

When you are comfortable, take more time and allow the meditation to heal any worries, bring light and love into your time, and regard it as your special place.

Ritual to Banish Negativity

It is a beautiful ritual to get rid of any negative relationships that are around you. Not just partnerships but work relationships or family. You can adapt this to help you heal and remove the negative impact past hurts have had.

Banishing Meditation for Getting Rid of Any Negative Relationships

As always, with meditating, ensure you are in a comfortable place with no distractions.

Have a pink or purple candle/tea light ready so that you can light it just before you begin. As you burn it, see the flame as a beacon and allow it to relax you.

You can place some crystals, such as rose quartz, in front of you.

Begin by sitting quietly in the moment and reflecting on your body. Place your hands in a comfortable position and breathe. Listen to your breath and feel that life-giving energy flow through your body.

Allow your tummy to move freely and regulate the pace of your breath.

Breathe ten times each time you feel your body release all its tension. Feel the pressure flow out of your body.

Visualise the person or situation causing you difficulties in front of you. Begin to say everything you wish to speak to them.

You hurt me, and you cheated on me. The disruption you have caused me impacted my life. The words must be your own.

Each time you say one of the hurts, release it and visualise it blowing away in the wind.

Begin to feel wonderful bright universal light flow down through your crown chakra at the top of your head. This fantastic, uplifting light will fill the gap that you have created.

Then, say three times, 'I thank you for the lessons you have shown me. I wish you well and send you on your way. I am ready to move on with my beautiful life and for a loving and fulfilling relationship.'

Start to release your body. Gently feel your feet and wriggle your toes. Massage your legs and stretch your arms. Roll your shoulders and feel yourself come round.

Keep the positive belief as you go forward.

Ritual for Releasing Negativity

Sometimes, meditation on its own is not enough when you have been through a significant trauma. A ritual will enhance this to clear negativity and the hurts of a previous relationship.

Take a bowl, candle paper, and a pen.

Write down everything you feel about the person or the situation you are carrying around with you – like baggage.

Place the paper in a bowl.

Burn what you have placed in the bowl.

'With the flames, I banish 'name' from my life. Go in peace and leave me in peace.

Bury the ashes with a black tourmaline crystal or some Epsom salts.

Now draw a bath and put in some Epsom Salts.

Wash your body with the salts and visualise removing all the negativity, pain, and residue that they have left on you.

Watch it all flow down the plug-hole

Ritual to Release the hold negative situations have had on you

Another way to undertake this type of release is to cut the cords binding you to a problem. Often, we only realise we have them once something happens, and it suddenly drags us down.

Regularly use a ritual to cord-cut from a broken heart or distressing incident or to remove the attachment that any person or situation may have remained attached to you. This type of ritual effectively helps challenges encountered in work situations.

Take sage and smudge your room or home. As you walk through, ask for all cords or any negativity to be removed. Ideally, have a window open to allow the air to flow freely.

Light a candle on your altar and place a photograph or a written description of what you wish to remove. It can even be a small drawing.

Place lavender and rose oil around the pictures.

Say all the things you want to say to the picture. Be bold and firm in what you say.

At the end, say I give gratitude and thanks for the lessons you have given me. Now, I cut the cords and move on with my life.

Take scissors and cut up the photograph or words.

Say, 'By my magic and love, I mend my pain. And cut the cord that bound me to you.

Snuff out the candle and cast the remnants of the photographs to the wind.

CHAPTER 9

Making the Best Decisions

Every minute of every day, we are faced with decisions about what to wear, what to eat, and some major ones about life-changing events. Indecision has the potential to cause you great difficulties in missed opportunities, or a lack of clarity makes you choose the wrong option. Then, you either must get out of it or live with it and try to patch up the turmoil that has been created. Here is some guidance on sound decision-making and some of the decisions you can make regularly. As always with this book, the decision to do anything is yours; this is your path and journey.

The aim is for you to make decisions that you are comfortable and confident with so it is something you can be proud of and not spend many sleepless nights worrying about. Many factors influence you and weave a web of distractions or attractive alternatives to take you away from the path you need to walk. Then you make the wrong decision. Try to avoid this and make sure you think about all the elements in a way that takes note of the following points.

- Ensure you only look at the facts from every direction that will support your end decision. Frequently, this is called confirmation bias.
- Leaping into making a decision about the first thing that comes to you and going with it is a premature decision or, in slang terms, 'A knee-jerk reaction.' We have all experienced this frequently and, to our regret,
- refuse to budge. No way will you move your viewpoint, whatever evidence or facts are presented. Even when you are proven to be completely wrong
- Looking on the bright side. Everything is hopeful and going beautifully, so from your viewpoint, it is seeing the good and ignoring everything else
- Fiddling with the facts. Believing the points in your mind are the correct ones or conveniently remembering things in a certain way and conveniently forgetting plenty of other things

- Only look at recent events and ignore the historical big picture that would provide you with a completely different perspective
- Family/Peer/Colleague influences. We have all experienced the manipulative effect of families. Where others are putting you in a position where you feel you must choose in a certain way as you do not want to upset them
- Selecting a practical option rather than what would be good for you holistically. Your spiritual wellbeing is more important than anything else. Most of the time, we hardly think about this
- Coaching/Mentoring will assist you with decision-making. They do not make the decisions for you but ask the right questions to help you choose the best option. We do supply this service, so please ask

Does this sound familiar? Our lives are made up of many choices. Individually, they do not amount to much, but adding them up over the years is immense. For example, always making the wrong buying choices – how much money would you have?

If you regret a decision you have made, most people will, so do not feel disheartened by it. You made that choice with bias or irrational thinking, and you need to take a positive step right now to change that. Only you can make that change.

What will help you to do this?

- Reflect on what you are doing. Make sure you think clearly and honestly
- Ask the questions 'What is motivating you to change jobs?', 'Do I need that pair of shoes?'
- Decide if you have a behavioural pattern. Sometimes, this can be difficult to spot, but if you journal or list some of your decisions, you may see a pattern emerging. Do you always buy black trousers and then buy more because you have convinced yourself you do not have any?

What about you?

So far, all the suggestions and ideas have been about processes or stages, things to think about. This section of the module is about what you need to do. This part is practical, and it will help if you can think of a decision you need to make and respond to the questions so that it has more meaning to you. Knowing and understanding more about you is also a good step forward, and reviewing how you work will provide insight into your situation and many parts of your life.

Exercise

Recognise that the following is an extended exercise and requires some thought. Decisions are essential daily, so understanding and feeling comfortable with this process is important.

Step one is to identify a decision that you need to make. The subject can be about anything.

Research, you need to commit to making that decision. Try saying, 'I am making this decision,' and name it; it can be about anything.

Understand if you are being flexible and taking note of all factors.

Are you scared of making the decision? The fear of making the wrong one is paralysing you about moving forward?

Are you prepared to challenge yourself to consider the decision positively, not taking yourself into a negative place?

How will you make the decision?

What are the implications if you do not make the decision?

How are you going to prioritise the details?

What are the implications if you do nothing?

Who will benefit from the decision?

What are the cost implications?

Intuitively, what do you think? Ask, 'Does this feel right?'

What is exciting about doing it?

What will you regret by not doing it?

You have been given a simple list, but reading it may require more time. As a task, apply it to something basic, such as purchasing a small item.

How you feel at any point in time significantly influences any decision you make, and you need to understand that it is when you reason and list the optimal decision that can be made. Separate emotion from feeling. Journal or record how you feel after using a decision-making process.

The Types of Decisions

Whatever the problem that you are encountering which requires a decision, it will fall into one of these three categories:

- Consumer Decision Making

Choosing what to purchase, ranging from something small to a considered purchase. It even comes down to your choice between tea or coffee at the end of a meal.

- Business Decision Making

You make a whole wealth of daily decisions in your business world. What to put in a report or whether or not to employ someone. The complexity of company changes or even what projects to initiate. If you cannot make good, solid decisions that you genuinely believe in, then the impact on others is immense and may influence your career.

- Personal Decision Making

Everything in your personal life. Get divorced, get married, buy a dog, what food shopping to get. To leave your job, start your own business, and know what car to buy. It also includes your investments and wisdom around financial management.

Each of these can follow the simple steps and enable you to make successful decisions about your work and personal life.

Mindful Decisions

There is a Chapter on the basics of mindfulness, which is an example of how to use it effectively to aid you when making critical decisions in your life. Be Mindful when you decide:

- Take things slowly; deliberate reflection creates clarity, so take stock of your talents and true interests or desires
- Accept that making a tough decision is not easy, especially if it is heart-wrenching. Embrace that it is a big decision and give it the time and consideration that it deserves
- Be your authentic self; only consider options that are genuinely aligned with what you believe and who you are
- Take the stress out of the decision and opt for the simple path. To do this, you need to identify what is best for you.

- Choose wisely when surrounded by multiple options, and by nurturing your soul and allowing it to breathe, that gut/intuitive decision will shine through.
- Take the path of least resistance. Even if you struggle to understand the universe and trust the way it is there, it will open to you. Just asking for support and guidance will help you gain universal clarity.
- If you are frightened as this is outside your comfort zone, stretch, listen to your body, and embrace it.
- Trust yourself. You know what the right path is. Choose it and stick to it
- Strive to be responsible, trustworthy, and kind. This does not mean shy away from making the difficult decisions but how you follow them through

CHAPTER 10

Spiritual Energy Healing

The spiritual body needs a particular type of care. We all know what visiting the doctor is about and understand it. Your spiritual wellbeing is different and significantly impacts your happiness, life, and how you approach relationships. It happily works alongside traditional medicines, and there is no suggestion that your medications should be dumped. This specialist type of healing works alongside and complements what you are already being treated for. This non-invasive type of healing works on a physical or emotional ailment by improving the immune system and glands through chakra work and some forms of depression, to name a few.

The question we all ask is – does it hurt? Healing energy is channelled through a healing medium (healer). They may be assisted by spirit guides or angels called in at the start to help. The laying on of hands and distant or absent healing are all ways healing can be provided to you. It is 'the transfer of energy from healer to recipient.'

The experience is a flow of light-bearing energy that may tingle or allow you to feel a great warmth; often, many colours are viewed in your mind's eye. During and after the healing, you feel a real inner peace and a strong sense of connection to the universe and that you are grounded.

At times of great loneliness, fear, grief, or stress are just a few of life's problems that would benefit from healing. Or if you want to relax deeply and peacefully. We usually feel better after visiting the hairdresser, so why not spoil your soul with a tailored treatment? Negative thoughts block your body's meridians, making you lose balance. Balancing and harmonising your soul will help you to be far more grounded and rational about what life throws your way.

This experience is part of your spiritual awakening. By taking the time to enjoy the energy you have given, you will see the benefits quickly become apparent in your daily life. It is vital to go to a qualified practitioner, and many freely share information about their experience. Choose the person you are drawn to and trust that feeling as it identifies what you need. Having faith in the healer and sharing your most important questions or struggles with them will bring a bond of trust between you.

Healing can mean different things, and there are many forms (listed are just a few). Getting to the root of the problem is a crucial place to start. So, be honest with yourself and the person trying to help you, however difficult it is for you.

Self-healing is an excellent first step. Simple, deep, and quality breathing will help alleviate anxiety. As mentioned, put your hand over your heart and welcome the beating rhythm. Forgiveness is a way of releasing and allowing yourself to be free from any past pain or trauma. Essential oils that you keep close and enjoy their scent when you need a boost. Or just breathing in the beautiful smells of nature.

Crystal healing incorporates the use of crystals. Usually, they will prescribe crystals that will help you daily. They will work on your chakra, as will many of the others. Reiki and the various types of this practice are the most popular and may involve the laying on of the practitioner's hands or holding just above you. Therapeutic touch, Massage, and Reflexology are all found at many spiritual events, or someone local to you will offer these services.

There is room for natural healing, and the accuracy with which it can identify the underlying source of your illness or feelings enables quality healing. Negative energy is present in so many people living in modern society. Ignoring the sideways glance from friends, you must be tired of the pressures of social media – the endless pictures saying, 'I am delighted.' Be honest with yourself. Constant pretence is not just putting immense conformity pressures on you but making you feel isolated. Healing is one way to put an end to this pain. Please help us to understand our souls, which is fundamental when on a spiritual journey, and get rid of that hollow pit of emptiness.

Exploring the different avenues or researching will be fun; you can learn and help yourself. Particularly about selecting crystals, indulging in their energy lets them focus on who you are and what you want.

CHAPTER 11

Mindfulness

What is Mindfulness?

Mindfulness is the ability to be fully present in where we are and what we are doing. By being present and understanding what is going on around you are not overwhelmed by it or have the temptation to overreact. It creates space between ourselves and our urge to react by breaking down conditioned responses. Frequently adopting this approach can enhance performance, gain insight into our minds, and significantly reduce stress.

It is not a fantasy or obscure and does not require us to change who we are fundamentally. It is helping us be the best of who we are, and it has become quite a transformational practice in business and personal development. Bringing awareness and caring into everything we do improves our lives and is only measurable once you look back and see what you were like before you adopted this into your routine. Anyone can do this; you do not have to be super fit or assume problematic poses.

Part of this involves meditation. This is not complex and gives you the deeply relaxing feeling of floating, and this is calming, allowing you to forget about any situations that cause you concern.

Some Basics to try

Set aside time; you do not need anything fancy, just quiet and the space to do this. If you lie down, there is a tendency to go to sleep.

Relax your body, and if possible, have the soles of your feet on the floor

Please pay attention to the present moment and observe it how it is. Have no judgment about what is going on – this sounds easy, but it will require time to adjust to thinking this way

If a decision does arise, let it pass by and flow around you without stopping. You may make a mental note but do not dwell on it.

Keep returning to the present moment; if you drift, return to the present.

If your mind wanders, do not judge whatever thoughts appear; gently bring yourself back.

The whole session does not need to take long, and even a few minutes will benefit you as you connect with your internal rhythms that are helping you relax. It is also a good way of helping to overcome injury. Make sure that whatever position you do this in is comfortable, as you need to be relaxed. You will be present now and not fearing what may happen in the future, so it is building your current strength.

Balance this with the other challenges this book has asked you to adopt, and you will find that this helps you with your confidence and esteem development.

CHAPTER 12

Spiritual Protection

The title may seem like a strange chapter, but spiritual protection is a positive way of helping you to feel confident. Most spiritual people will use some form of protection. Ways include using crystals or putting some form of energy field around you. Within the spiritual world, there is far more to this, which is fascinating.

You may have heard the term 'grounding, and it's a term that causes confusion but is about your stability. Being grounded ensures that anyone who says or does something hostile towards you, even unintentionally, will not destabilise you. If you are not grounded, then it does have the potential to make you anxious or overthink the situation. Visualise a mighty oak tree, hundreds of years old, with a vast root structure. It will take a big wind to blow that over. A tree with flimsy roots is quickly a victim of the wind. So, daily, make sure you feel grounded, stable, and ready to face the day.

In your everyday lives, the psychology of putting protection around you is uplifting. You can walk forward confidently (not arrogantly) and know you are protected. Knowing you have your invisible armour, the thought of going to a meeting at work will do wonders for your self-belief. Or when someone throws you 'a look,' be confident it cannot pierce your shield.

There are people often called 'energy vampires'; it is their mission to drain all of your energy and wear you down. They can be highly damaging, and you struggle to stay awake or maintain your focus. Others are in a situation where they are drawing your energy, not realising it, and giving you some negativity in return!

Make some of this part of your daily routine.

- If you feel there is something dark, shine a light on it. People or situations that are unsettling or something you are unsure of. Imagine pouring bright, vibrant light at it.
- Use candles; it is not so easy at work, but at home, soften the edges of your home.

- Place a bright white light shield around you, or imagine you are in a personal reflective bubble.
- Increase your vibration
- Or use some crystals. If you ask, you will be amazed at how many of your friends carry crystals.

Using some form of protection is a personal choice and needs to be a conscious decision to make daily rather than as and when you feel like it.

Other people carry a mascot or good luck charm; these need to mean something to you, as when you need that little extra support, you must trust and believe that it will be there to support you.

Exercise

Think of a time when someone said or did something that destroyed your balance. Not physically, but the spoken word that came from nowhere and had a huge impact. Would it have had the same result if you had a level of protection around you and felt grounded? Write down your thoughts and how you will use protection going forward.

TIME FOR YOUR JOURNEY

Thank you for being part of this book, reading it, and hopefully working through some exercises. Taking part and reflecting on some of the challenges will all add to your development and allow the amazing you to shine through.

Opening the door will enable you to walk forward confidently and be completely comfortable with who you are. Loving yourself is at the root of everything you do, so take the time to get that right, and the rest will follow.

'Only from the heart can you touch the sky.'

Rumi

ABOUT THE AUTHOR

Liz has been involved in the spiritual world for most of her life. During her corporate job, she met many people trying to make sense of their daily lives and manage that balance between life and work. When poor health, or as she jokes, 'The Universe gave me a new path', stopped her in her tracks, she had a change in direction.

She works as a Spiritual Guidance Coach, Crystal Healer and Tarot Reader. She has helped people worldwide and worked with incredible mentors and guides and is now passing on that knowledge. Liz regularly makes short TV and radio appearances at events and on social media. Her other books on love and tarot, along with her oracle cards, are regularly used by others in their spiritual journeys. She regularly holds courses and workshops and looks after the Crystal Shack Academy.

Bringing spiritual and life path information in an easy-to-read and understandable way is essential as is helping people to make a real difference in their lives.

Thanks to my husband, daughter and friends for their support.

Special thanks to Mark Duffin, an incredible artist for the cover painting. See more of his work on markduffin.net

Milton Keynes UK
Ingram Content Group UK Ltd.
UKHW010146140324
439402UK00012B/132